WHY PRESIDENT OBAMA LOST THE 2012 ELECTION:
A Wake-Up Call

By

Jim Green

DEDICATED TO:

Tod [who suggested I write this book]

ISBN-13: 978-1478397564

ISBN-10: 147839756X

Prologue:

The 2012 election has yet to take place as I write—but if President Obama does lose, I will be one of the most disappointed—

Not only because I am a cheerleader—but also because it will mean that America is finished!

After being plundered when the Republicans have held the White House over the past 30 years, America cannot handle another round of Republican's "lie, cheat, and rob" to get elected, so they can "lie, cheat and rob" America blind—once elected!

Indeed, Romeny, Limbaugh, Bockmann, Ryan, etc., —the gang—have sanctioned a level of lying unheard of in prior elections--To borrow from Gore Vidal—"Lying to someone who is dying, by saying they look good, is good manners—but lying to get elected is dangerous"—and for the current crop of Republicans--if their lips are moving, they are lying!

And, it is time for Americans to start identifying these persons for what they are—"Not Decent People"—[decent people would never do what they are doing]--And as we add MD to the end of a medical doctor's name--we need to henceforth add NDP to the name of every Republican to whom this applies—starting with the "gang", above....for instance, Paul Ryan, NDP....and the GOP has been traded for NDP....

And the Akin debacle in Missouri [Akin and Ryan co-sponsored "personhood" legislation, even if it was the result of rape—which their legislation re-defined to minimize]—and which underscores in red just how far the Republican Party has fallen into this abyss, which rebukes modernity, science and critical thinking! The Republican Party has sold its soul in their desperation to pursue the anti-Christian agenda—of GREED, just for the sake of GREED--and forgotten the adage "Lay down with dogs, and get up with fleas" [and no apology regarding the definition of anti-Christian hypocrites—if one is not following the teachings of Christ—they are NOT a Christian]¹

Regarding our unemployment crisis, Howard Schultz, CEO of Starbucks, makes a great cup of coffee—but he doesn't know beans [no pun intended] about how to fix our unemployment crisis—and this is cited because Mr. Schultz, and with every good intention, started "Create Jobs for USA". Problem is, he is still looking to the market to solve this problem….The dilemma for the business community is that while every waking moment in capitalism is spent pondering how to eliminate as many of us humans, as possible, from the workplace—to increase profits—what can't be ignored is the Halo effect high unemployment has on consumer confidence--people stop buying the products made by the business community--when we have high unemployment….

Thus, the bottom line is, and a major question asked in this book—HOW DO WE FIX OUR UNEMPLOYMENT CRISIS?

And, in part, the purpose of this book is to provide the answer.

Writing this book as a post-mortem, however, is a vehicle to look at issues from the perspective of "hindsight is 20-20" —and as Oscar Wilde averred "The only truly worthless opinion, is an unbiased one."—so what you will read, here, is my analysis of how we got where we are—and what we need to do to solve our problems in a 21st Century world—

Finally, here—I published my first book on my 78th birthday—and I have published one a month, on average, since [this is the 5th]—not that I write that fast, or well—they are all compilations of writings gathering dust over the past 30 years—

and with a growing outrage how we are becoming a plutocracy or oligarchy, take your pick—

And to protect this tiny handful of rulers [and while claiming to be the most free country on earth]—we have had an explosion in prison building over this 30 years—passing up every other nation on earth in prison population by 1990, and we now have more Americans in prison than any other civilized country in the world—we have the same prison population as China—But they have a billion more people! Specifically, we now have 5% of the world's population, and 25% of all prison inmates on earth in our prisons!

And this is due in large part because we [Republicans and Democrats, alike—albeit, Republicans by far the worst offender] are unwilling or unable to create programs that will solve our unemployment crisis!

Yes, we have NO job creation program in America—real job creation, either proposed [except HR 870]--or on the books!

That is, we have never looked at unemployment as a "stand alone" social problem—but rather it is seen as a step-child to market recovery—i.e., if the market fails, the unemployed are out of luck! More on this shortly—

Finally, a note to the reader—if you are a "typo-wonk"—are more concerned with sentence structure, etc., than content—you probably won't like my writing—and a wayward capital letter, here and there, and appearing out of place and used for emphasis—editorial license—so apologies, here—just look for content, please….THX

Chapter One

THE HISTORY OF HOW WE GOT WHERE WE ARE:

In the mid-1970's, the colliding forces of automation, technology, globalization, etc., reached a critical mass, resulting in ubiquitous unemployment in all of the OECD countries, and has left their leaders conflicted, ever since, regarding the displaced employee—Eurozone unemployment is still in double digits, with Spain at 22.9%, and with high youth unemployment a major factor in Arab Spring.

In the U.S., we took a pro-active role in addressing, and as a direct response to this economic shift—and in 1978 President Carter signed into law 15 USC § 3101--which "authorizes" the creation of a "reservoir of public employment" at any time our unemployment in America exceeds "3%".

The following year, in 1979, however, and in a panic over Humphrey-Hawkins—our ultra-conservative foundations, and desperate to preserve the "market only" job creation concept, embraced a flawed paper by an obscure MIT student, David L. Birch "The Job Generation Process"; and [with lots of cash] gave his paper biblical importance, and every president since has cited his finding as gospel.

Birch's paper concluded that "small businesses" were the greatest generator of new jobs—problem is, for the purposes of policy-making—it is BS. In a study at Harvard University in 2010, "The Myth of Small Business Job Creation" The research shows "no systematic relationship between firm size and growth." And that small businesses can actually detract from job growth—nevertheless, it is still the Republican One and Only job creation solution!

And in spite of this Washington struggles, still, to make this antiquated and unworkable notion, work--that it is only the market that can create jobs—the world has changed, our solutions haven't, and the result has been a disaster, politically as well as otherwise!

It would be impossible to still have 8.3% unemployment if we were on the right path [the result is the proof]—and among other problems with this concept--if the market fails, the unemployed are out of luck [It is the reason Romeny's job creation solution is a farce!].

Further, unemployment is a "social" problem we are seeking to address with a highly unstable, incompatible entity: The Market --That is, the last place we should look for a reliable solution to our unemployment crisis is The Market....

And, what apparently isn't clear going forward in the 21st Century, is that an expanding and contracting public workforce is an INDISPENSABLE component to the correct functioning of a modern market economy—i.e., The Humphrey-Hawkins Full Employment Act was dead-on correct in 1978—and provided a "win-win" solution for America--

The market thrives when we have a robust, employed, consuming workforce, and it is essential to consumer confidence—and overlooked is that HR 870 [currently in Committee], and the proposed "Neighbor-To-Neighbor Job Creation Act" [hereafter NTN] See: www.Inclusivism.org [both authorized under Humphrey-Hawkins], are deficit-neutral--Pro-Market "win-win" solutions: The American people win, and capitalism wins—

Chapter Two

THE MYTHS AND GOBLINS THAT HINDER OUR PROGRESS

The damage caused by our high unemployment is almost incalculable—for the business community as well as the unemployed--and it would be impossible to have 8.3% [almost one in 10 Americans] unemployed—if we were on the right path to fix this extremely serious social/economic/political problem—

And the problem, in large part, is because unemployment is _not_ addressed as a stand–alone "social" problem—but rather, is seen as a step-child to market recovery—and the obvious downside to this mind-set--if the market fails, the unemployed are out of luck!

Former editor of the Harvard Business Review, Dr. David Ewing, in his book "Freedom Inside The

Organization" [1977] observed "Employee rights are like a black hole in space, so impacted by tradition that light can barely escape.".

And it is these "traditions" [and loaded with myths] that we need to drill down on so that we can both analyze why we are where we are—and also so we can bring our "job creation" into the 21st Century.

For instance, the panic by the untra-right foundations in 1979, noted above, and their desperate efforts to undermine Humphrey-Hawkins is from the deeply held belief and tradition that the American "employee" is to be drawn from "a pool of slaves" to be used and discarded "at will".

In short, they still have one foot firmly planted on the plantation….

And this also explains their systematic destruction of unions in America, and the millions they have spent enacting "Right To Work" laws in 24 of our 50 states [the title of these laws a joke, of course]—because they have nothing to do with the "right to work", but rather the elimination of unions in these states—so that "employees" can be drawn from a pool of slaves to be used and discarded "at will"….

In short, we have a very steep hill to climb to bring us into the 21st Century—and particularly when we have tens of millions of dollars being spent to keep us on the plantation…

Another irony in the misnomer "Right To Work" states--when we superimpose the map over the "red vs blue" states the match is eerily similar— Those states with Right To Work laws are almost all red, and vice-versa.

Also compounding this is a lack of understanding [having the wool being pulled over their eyes]--on the part of a gullible public, to use an environment metaphor.

It is transparent why our "profiteers" want to eliminate the EPA, and driven by pure GREED—so they can drill the Rocky Mountains down to an ant hill—but the "rank and file" support this plunder of our earth for a single reason. Jobs

That is, persons who by all that is right should not be anti-environment—Are so immersed in the tradition that jobs can only be created by the Market, i.e., the belief that they wouldn't be able to get a job unless we go along with this plunder—so they too, would destroy the planet for a "good paying job"—a tragic dilemma for mother Earth, and us inhabitants!

Another irony, is that "most [Americans think] that anybody willing to work should be able to find a job" a quote from the "The Audacity of Hope" –the quote goes on to add "that paid a living wage."—but this is a given, and not that the minimum wage laws are the answer but they protect against exploitation.

What is most interesting about this quote, however, is that we are a democracy and if most Americans believe that "anybody willing to work should be able to find a job" [86% according to a recent Zogby poll]—where are our laws to make it a reality?

In short, the American people are saying fix unemployment, and this will in turn fix the economy—rather than the other way around—a point not lost on the "occupy" movement....

And, under the "authorization" in Humphrey-Hawkins at no time should our unemployment in America exceed "3%".

To understand why our unemployment is not now at 3%, we need to drill down on our solutions being "so impacted by tradition that light can barely escape.".

For instance, and to dissect two separate interviews:

On GPS, on January 29, 2012, Timothy Geithner stated in response to the question from Fareed Zarkaria, when we could expect jobs to return, Mr. Geithner strapped the solution to our unemployment crisis to "How fast we grow", i.e., how fast the market [our economy] grows—AND, in an interview on CNN of August 3, 2012, and in response to the same question, Austan Goolsbee responded "Jobs are tied to the economy".

The responses are linked together because they are both saying the same thing—their responses are coming from the same mind-set.

Mr. Geithner and Mr. Goolsbee, are our brightest and best—they went to our best schools--Mr. Geithner is the current United States Secretary of the Treasury, Mr. Goolsbee is former Chairman of the Council of Economic Advisers to President Obama.

In neither interview did the respondents say I am very sorry to say that our only means to create jobs in America is via market recovery—because both believe that our current methodology is correct— i.e., our hands a tied and current economic theory will not allow us to think outside the "conventional wisdom" box—

That is, in looking at unemployment as a stand-alone "social" problem—that MUST be solved independent of, and separate from the market— but this is not even on the table, indeed, even on the radar—neither of these gentlemen, however, are ill-willed, or ill-intentioned—they are just wrong….

Mostly, they don't understand the problem they have been asked to solve—for instance, if the federal government [the CDC] took the same approach in the AIDS crisis—as the federal government, to date, has taken in solving our unemployment crisis—we would still have tens of thousands dying from this dread disease!

And anyone believing that the Republicans, and particularly Romney, thinks any differently, or even has a clue--is from another planet! Indeed, Romney believes this archaic mind-set is the word of God!

In short, this antiquated mind-set is "conventional wisdom" in America—and it is why we have 25 million Americans unemployed, or underemployed! And lest we forget— "conventional wisdom" once held that the world was flat—[and world travel was out of the question]....and it needs to be challenged, in this instance—BECAUSE IT DOESN'T WORK! The result is the proof....

The really sad conclusion to this chapter, however, is that had the Democrats [when they had the opportunity], in fact, given "job creation" the social/economic/political importance it should have had—and reduced unemployment to 3%--the Tea Party would be meeting in a phone booth--the 2010 election would not have been a disaster--and all the good work of the Obama administration would have been Bulletproof, rather than as it has turned out: A Target

Chapter Three

WHAT WE NEED TO DO GOING FORWARD IN THE 21ST CENTURY:

Inexplicably "public employment" is seen the same as WPA—where millions are employed directly by the federal government—when that model is not only outmoded—it is insufficient to address our problems in the 21st century.

What we need today is an expanding and contracting public workforce—that expands during downturns in the market, and contracts as employees return to the private sector [Google: The Buffer Stock Employment Model]—triggered anytime our unemployment exceeds "3%" [as "authorized" under Humphrey-Hawkins]--and least understood: This is an INDISPENSABLE component in the effective functioning of our 21st Century Market.

The market thrives when we have a robust, employed, consuming workforce—our manufacturers are sitting on $2 trillion in cash because they do not have consumers for their products—i.e., absent consumers, they lay off employees—[and the Republican solution, Reaganomics, has acted as an accelerate to this downward spiral—and which Romney promises to return us to if he is elected]!

In short, the above model is a "win-win" solution—the American people win, and capitalism wins!

To achieve this, what is being urged is "The Neighbor-To-Neighbor Job Creation Act"; A federally mandated, mutual insurance—owned by our employed [from janitor to CEO] to create a fund to hire/train our unemployed.

To be viable, however, our job creation solution _MUST_ contain:

1] Be based on the premise that we have far more work that needs to be done in America, than we have persons to fill these jobs.

2] It MUST have renewable funding.

3] It will not add a dime to our deficit.

To expand briefly, it is currently believed, erroneously, that we need "make work" jobs so that everyone who wants to work will have a job—but this is absurd—and an insult to "Yankee Ingenuity".

We do not have an unemployment crisis from a shortage of jobs, or money—but rather from a shortage of imagination.

Regarding "renewable funding" ALL of our job creation solutions, to date, have been based on the mind-set: "jump start" the market, and the market will in turn create all the jobs we need—and even setting aside that this is untrue, our current job creation is moving at a snail's pace—long past the unemployment benefits drying up—with the CBO projecting that even with the JOBS Act, signed into law on April 6, 2012--it will be 2017 before we return to a barely acceptable 5.5% unemployment rate!

Further, by its nature when we "jump start" --the employment ends when the funding runs out as we learned from the Stimulus—whereas any real fix to our unemployment crisis _demands_ renewable funding....

And whether the electorate will accept an unemployment rate hovering around 8% on election day—is the $64,000 question....

Regarding not adding a dime to our deficit—under The Neighbor-To-Neighbor Job Creation Act [NTN], the *funding* to reduce our unemployment to 3% comes from an insurance owned by our employed, rather than added to our deficit—

If one is employed in America, participation in this insurance plan is mandatory—similar in concept to our auto insurance or Social Security Insurance [and without question the most successful social program in American history].

Jobs beget jobs--And with a modest policy cost of 4% of salary we can create more "private-sector" jobs in 6 months, that HR 2847, and the JOBS Act, in 6 years—and unlike these laws—NTN will not add a dime to our deficit!

Finally, this is in total concert with the will of the American people, i.e., that "anybody willing to work should be able to find a job"—and the

American people have told our politicians time and again of their willingness to chip in to help their neighbor get a job [and as an *insurance*, as above, it also protects their continued employment]—it is just that Washington is deaf as an adder!

Chapter Four

THE BLUEPRINT FOR MAKING NTN
OPERATIONAL

We have one member of Congress who has a hand on the pulse of the American people, regarding the subject at hand, and is of like-mind with the concept presented, here [albeit his funding is slightly different] —John Conyers from Michigan,

And every Congressional session Representative Conyers introduces an updated version of Humphrey-Hawkins, only to watch it die in Committee—it is currently HR 870, and currently in Committee in the House.

The primary difference between NTN--the proposed, above, and HR 870, is how it is funded—with HR 870 funded with a small fee on transactions on the stock market—i.e., the funding would come from Wall Street. Both, however, address our current 21ˢᵗ Century dilemma--that the world has changed, our solutions haven't, and the result has been a disaster....

The following is the blueprint for implementation of The Neighbor-To-Neighbor Job Creation Act:

1] The Department of Labor would create a National Trust Fund, with funds to be received from existing FICA accounts, and supplemented, if needed, from a windfall profits tax on excessive profits, for instance, by our major oil corporations, etc.

2] A Commission would be set up within the Department of Labor to review grant requests from every jurisdiction in America, including but not limited to states, local governments, Indian tribes, but specifically rejecting "privatization" requests [which historically have cut services to increase profits—and notorious for "cronyism"].

3] The target would be to reduce unemployment to no more than 3% nationally within one year of enactment, i.e., to not more than 3% for persons 20, or over, and not more than 4% for persons 16 or over—and as currently authorized under the Humphrey-Hawkins Full Employment Act [15 USC § 3101]

4] Further, grant funds would be distributed to authorized jurisdictions to train persons for gainful employment.

5] The funding of projects would be bifurcated, i.e., identified as a "national" or "local" project— with national projects, for example, a high-speed rail system, space exploration, alternative energy projects—[Today half of the world's population lives in a megalopolis--"In 1950, there was only one city with a population of more than 10 million—New York City—today, there are 21, and the number of urban areas with populations between five and ten million has shot from 7 to 37." National Geographic, November 2002].

6] Local grant requests could include: Child care for low income families, the urgent need outlined by the NEA for School Modernization, long over-due infrastructure repair, the creation of Federal Regional Diagnostic and Treatment Centers for the diagnosis and treatment of the violent offender— the list of social benefits is almost endless.

7] To the greatest degree possible this Act would be carried out under the over-arching Buffer Stock Employment Model, where public employment would expand during downturns in the market [and triggered at 3% unemployed, as "authorized" under H-H], and contract as employees return to the private sector.

Chapter Five

ECONOMIC INCLUSIVISM: A 21st Century Solution

"There is one thing stronger than all the armies in the world, and that is an idea whose time has come" Victor Hugo

Economic Inclusivism is Neo-Capitalism—Inclusive pro-market solutions to our social problems.

We are in the throes of enormous socio-economic change, and all of the above in this book is a component in a larger, more comprehensive roadmap, I have identified as *Economic Inclusivism*—and which poses the question:

What solutions do we need to apply going forward in a 21st Century world?

It may be too cynical, but many of the solutions today could be compared to pouring gasoline on a fire to put it out....

For one, our insane incarcerate rate—which has made American more dangerous, not less—and undermines the education of our youth; and adding to our deficit with "jump start" job creation—with the jobs ending the minute the funding runs out—and has resulted a cost-effective nightmare....

Our starting point for Economic Inclusivism is based on a truism, and asserted by every credible economist: "High and persistent unemployment has pervaded almost every OECD country since the mid-1970s."— Dr. William F. Mitchell, Economist

So given this reality—what adjustments do we need to make?

Many of our solutions, today, are based on applying the "rules" that applied prior to this cosmic shift in our economy—but like "Pouring new wine into old wineskins"—to borrow from scripture [I'm an agnostic]—the result has been a disaster....

In short, the following bifurcated solutions are devoid of an ideological agenda—and are based, solely, on being EFFECTIVE solutions:

Economic Reforms

1] Work must become a legal right. To address our insidious practice of "exclusion", Congress must enforce a citizen's legal right to work, as enacted by Congress in "The Full Employment Act of 1946", and as outlined in the Democratic National Platform position asserting "Opportunity to every American". We need to recognize that the right to work and be a productive member of one's society is a human right, as an adjunct to the free enterprise system. Additionally, we need to set in motion the following constitutional amendment: "Work shall hereafter be the legal right of every citizen, and Congress shall, except for retirement/disability programs under federal jurisdiction, make no laws which will abridge the right of any citizen of legal age, to work and be a productive citizen".

2] To ensure enforcement/fund this legal right, Congress would create a federally mandated, mutual insurance--owned by our employed to provide a fund to hire/train our unemployed [outlined in detail, above].

3] Since this program of "inclusion" would address 95% of our social ills (crime, welfare, drugs, etc., and exacerbated in many cases by inept Band-Aid programs), the federal budget could be greatly reduced and our current Federal

Income Tax would be replaced with a National Sales Tax, value-added tax, a national lottery, or some combination of taxes other than our current Federal Income Tax. Billions are spent annually trying to get around the Tax Code, all of which is passed on to us, the consumer, in the higher cost of consumer goods.

Social/Prison Reforms

4] We need to re-classify all crime in the future as violent or non-violent, and discard the archaic terms felony and misdemeanor. The term "felony" is fixed in the public's mind as "armed and dangerous"—and yet over 70% of our prison inmates are in prison for non-violent offenses [50% are in for drug related offenses]—and if for no other reason this undermines our intelligently addressing the real problem: The violent offender.

5] We need a much greater use of "Shock" Incarceration [a concept I authored in the 1960's];

a greater use of fines and probation [both civil and criminal], in lieu of incarceration, and an expanded menu of sentencing alternatives. Prison should be a last resort, not first, and through the above social re-structuring we will have far less need for incarceration.

6] We need the creation of Federal Regional Diagnostic and Treatment Centers, for the diagnosis and treatment of the violent offender [And given the recent spate of assaults in Aurora and Wisconsin—and the urgent need to restore the ban on assault weapons—how about a ban on the NRA leadership!]....

7] We need to pick-up the lead taken by England, in treating drug addiction as a "medical" rather than a "criminal" problem, so that we can effectively curb drug-related crime, and keep drugs out of the hands of our youth.

8] A universal healthcare system is an indispensable component of a sane society. We are the only major industrial country in the world without universal healthcare—and we pay twice as much, for half the result [only a slight exaggeration] for our healthcare in America—We are ranked 37th in the world in healthcare by the World Health Organization.

Chapter Six

HOW MUCH SHOULD YOU PAY, HOW MUCH SHOULD I PAY?

The raging issue going on in America, today, turns on this single question—and since 1980 we started seeing more and more tax watchdog groups cropping up all over the place—some by persons who would starve to death if others didn't pay theirs—[Hint: The Tea Party folk]

The driving force behind this demonizing the payment of taxes are the Koch brothers—a slight exaggeration, and slightly unfair—but used here as a metaphor for that tiny, tiny handful, the 400 who now hold more of America's wealth than 50% of the rest of us Americans—and a direct result of their getting Bush II appointed to the presidency!

In fact, a larger question is when does spending billions in propaganda to keep from paying taxes, cease to be cost-effective? And apparently the 1% haven't reached that point yet—but one thing is obvious and that is that their "allegiance is to money", rather than their "allegiance to America"--after all, most got their wealth from us—the 99%--the American people!

And it should be transparent to anyone voting in this election that when these folks want to spend a billion dollars plus to get Romney elected—that the last person us 99% should vote for--is Romney....

The only question we should have on the table in this election is: What kind of America do we want for ourselves? So use your brains, folks—VOTE to re-elect President Obama!

Chapter Seven

FILLING IN THE BLANK SPOTS: Miscellaneous
papers and letters

COMMONS SENSE ECONOMICS:

- We cannot siphon America's wealth away from
  the consuming middle without causing
  economic collapse—[1987 & 2008—i.e.,
  Supply-Side has a shelf-life of about 7 years]--
- When every waking moment in capitalism is
  spent pondering ways to eliminate as many of
  us humans, as possible, from the workplace—to
  increase profits—why on earth would anyone
  look to this model to solve an unemployment
  crisis?
- Unemployment is a "social" problem—and "our
  government" has an absolute responsibility to
  step forward with a viable solution.

- We should never condemn the CEO who closes a plant when they are losing money—but we should be outraged by a government that is indifferent or incompetent in finding a viable solution to the resulting "social" problem.
- Capitalism thrives when we have a robust, employed, consuming public—
- "Public-sector" jobs is an accelerate to "private-sector" jobs—and will create more "private-sector" jobs in 6 months, than HR 2847 The HIRE Act, in 6 years, if ever—
- The belief that "public-sector" jobs can only be created by increasing the deficit, or equals a massive government program, such as WPA—is a belief that is suffering from a lack of imagination—
- The Humphrey-Hawkins Full Employment Act which authorizes the creation of a "reservoir of public employees" anytime our unemployment in America rises above "3%" is a Pro-Market solution—and an INDISPENSABLE tool for economic survival in a modern market

economy—See also HR 870 [currently in Committee]--

- In the mid-1970's—the colliding forces of automation, globalization, innovation, etc., reached a critical mass, resulting in ubiquitous unemployment—and has left our leaders befuddled with what to do with the displaced employee?

- Our response in America was H-H, above, in 1978—but inexplicably never implemented—and the resulting high unemployment cost Carter the election in 1980--

- "Most [Americans think] that anybody willing to work should be able to find a job." President Obama, "The Audacity of Hope" – it is not the American people standing the in the way our implementing H-H—it is bad advice—

- The correlation between high unemployment and our lethargic economy is absolute—

- A comprehensive public employment program, in compliance with H-H, such a HR 870, or a federally mandated, mutual insurance, owned

by America's employed--to hire/train our
unemployed [www.Inclusivism.org]. Is Pro-
Market, and pro-the American people--

Jim Green, Democrat candidate for Congress,
2000

President Obama/Fellow Democrats:

"Conservative" is the big word in Republican parlance in this election—and the candidates stumble all over themselves to say it as many times possible is their 30 second ads--

Indeed, Romney referred to himself as "severely conservative" and even declared that he was "more conservative than Rick Santorum" [which is way out there]—and he went on to say "I'm not concerned about the very poor".

But in drilling down on this a bit—the Republican candidates are obviously trying to appeal to persons who embrace being "conservative"—but what does this mean?

There are different ways to be conservative—a person can be fiscally conservative, and be socially "liberal", or vice-versa—but you get the sense that "severely conservative" is code for I'm not a "liberal".

And after years of Republicans demonizing the word "liberal" in their propaganda ads--it is little wonder that in their prayers at night their followers thank God they are not a "liberal"—

But those who define themselves as "conservative" might do well to look up the definition of the antonym for the word "liberal"--"illiberal" in Webster's.

And the real shocker for those who are slaves to the labels, i.e., propaganda buzz words, in this election will be shocked to learn that if they buy car insurance—they are a "socialist"—

Yep folks, our car insurance is based on the same collectivist principle as "socialism"—we pool our money to protect us when fate taps us on the shoulder—

And communism differs only in that it is controlled by a totalitarian state dominated by a single and self-perpetuating political party, which, of course, is also its fatal flaw.

Indeed, it is this flaw that has made the extremes on both the right and the left--fascism and communism, fail. It takes a dictator to hold the government in place—and it is the antithesis of a democracy.

In sum, what we need is a "post-label" election—to cut out the noise so the electorate will actually listen what the candidates are saying.

For instance, when Romney says that he wants to cut taxes for the 1% ever further it is consummate proof that he intends to return to the same failed policies that took America, and our economy straight over a cliff!

Jim Green, Democrat candidate for Congress, 2000

President Obama/Fellow Democrats:

For the past 65 years we have had two parallel paths to address unemployment in America—

To assure employment for the troops returning from WW II, President Truman signed into law The Full Employment Act of 1946—

This was expanded upon in 1978 with the Humphrey-Hawkins Full Employment Act, signed into law by President Carter—

And a 21st Century version of this path to full employment in America, is pending the House, HR 870.

Humphrey-Hawkins best defines this path to addressing unemployment in America, and it "authorizes" our government to create a "reservoir of public employees" anytime our unemployment rises above "3%".

And in spite of the fact that this path to employment has been the law of the land since 1946—and is a Pro-Market solution [more on this shortly]---Washington has lacked the wherewithal to implement this path to employment on behalf of the American people—[a point not lost on the "occupy" movement].

Rather, Washington has taken the alternate parallel path—by insisting that human labor is a "component" in the free enterprise system—[barely distinguishable from the machine the human operates] to be used and discarded "at will"—and the Republican propaganda is that it is an attack upon "freedom" to challenge this concept, but whose "freedom"?

As a result, however, "conventional wisdom" has insisted that it is the market, alone, that can fix our unemployment crisis—the result has been a disaster—

The market thrives when we have a robust, employed, consuming public—and by taking this parallel path—we not only have a staggering 8.1% unemployment, but a struggling recovery as well.

Ironically, following WW II, Australia passed a law very similar to our Full Employment Act of 1946—

Difference is—they actually put it into effect—and over the next 30 years—[until the cold winds of conservatism swept in Reagan and Thatcher, etc.] –the government in Australia saw as a solemn responsibility that "anyone willing to work should be provided with a job" [a quote from the "Audacity of Hope"].

The citizens of Australia still refer to this 30 years as their "Golden Age".

Jim Green, Democrat candidate for Congress,
2000   www.Inclusivism.org

Letter to editor/NY Times:

It is a mystery to me why no one is raising the issue that the billions our corporations make in "profits"—creates, at a minimum, a fiduciary obligation to those who brought them these [in some cases obscene] "profits":

It is US, folks—You and me—the American people—the 99%, if you will--and this also creates a fiduciary obligation for the betterment of society—

But these obligations goes out the window when it comes to the corporate Super Pacs—where a GREEDY few are pouring in millions of the dollars they got from us—not for the betterment of America, or the American people—

But rather for their personal aggrandizement—Greed, just for the sake of greed--and at the expense of the economic well being of the 99%!

Further, greed, for the sake of greed is antithetical to Christ's teachings! Indeed, the Republican One and Only program is to pander to the GREED of their wealthiest contributors!

What a double-cross—using our money to stick it to us!

And now with the worst decision from the U.S. Supreme Court since the Dred Scott Decision [which set the stage for our Civil War]—the "Citizens United" decision—this corporate cash can be given in secret, and in unlimited amounts!

Further, with Romney in his daily rants against President Obama, asserting that President Obama doesn't know "When to send jobs overseas"—how much of that cash is coming for Romeny from Indonesia, or Singapore, or China?

Our elections are now for sale to the highest bidder—and we are subjected to a blizzard of propaganda ads on the internet—written by corporate slugs pretending to be legitimate—and paid for by these Super Pacs [our money]!

Surely, everyone can see through this internet BS, can't they? Don't answer that—

Jim Green

So long as the potential for manipulation of electronic voting continues to exist—our elections in America will be in peril! In spite of all the polls showing a strong Obama victory--it was not until 10PM Central on 11-4-08.....that we could breath a sigh of relief....we had been cheated out of the past two elections....with many believing that Bush was never legally elected president of the United States....and we were braced for the worst.......this can, and MUST be fixed before 2012, so that this never happens again, and in the interest of all who support fair and open elections--regardless of party. Accordingly, it is urged that we adopt the following proposed "FAIL-SAFE ELECTRONIC VOTING ACT":

THE FAIL-SAFE ELECTRONIC VOTING ACT

1) EVERY electronic voting machine (hereafter EVM), must be inexpensive, identical throughout the U.S. in a 1/150 ratio, and *must count and produce a hard-copy of the recorded votes*. In

addition, an extra copy of their recorded votes would be produced (not necessarily a hard-copy), marked "Voter's Copy", and containing "NOTICE: Do Not Destroy Until Every Election On Your Ballot Is Certified". [If Wal-Mart refused to give us a receipt for our purchases—would they not be suspect—and this regards our democracy].

2) *After confirming that their votes are recorded correctly,* the voter would then insert the hard-copy ballot into a software-free (count only) optical scanner (hereafter OS), for a second count. The hard-copy ballot would be retained by election officials in the event a candidate asks for a recount (*not possible under the current system, and which undermines the legality of each such election).* The EVM and the OS must be manufactured by different companies (which is universally true today).

3) Election officials assigned to oversee the EVM, would be prevented by law from overseeing the

OS, and vice-versa, and stiff criminal penalties would be imposed for violations.

4) Further, every EVM would be programmed with raw data re the total registration rolls, by party, and norms for their voting history, etc.,----as an "alert" to a possible irregularity, such as an "Under-vote"—or "vote-flipping" etc., and _standards_established to suspend certification where there is an "improbable result", at least temporarily, of a particular election until the discrepancy is cleared up. (This is what computers do best, and it would be very easy to create such a program).

5) At the end of the election day, tallies would be taken from the EVM and the OS, for each candidate. _If the tallies didn't balance for any given election, or if there is an "alert", that election cannot be certified until the "error" is corrected._ If the candidates agree (the victory is certain), minor discrepancies in the count could be disregarded.

While probably rare, the Voter, or a random sample of Voters, would be required by law to return their Copy of the recorded votes to the election office to clear up any "error", or where an "alert" signals the need for same.

6) Further, every state provides for a recount when the total vote falls below a certain percent of difference between the candidates, impossible to conduct with the current EVM—and thus Congress must mandate the following regarding presidential candidates: A RUN-OFF election is mandated and triggered in those states where the percent of total vote is less than .5% of difference between any given candidates; said election to be held on the second Saturday following the election, on PAPER BALLOTS ONLY, and contain ONLY the names of the relevant candidates, for instance: "Barack Obama, Democrat" and "John McCain, Republican"—with oversight in counting by a representative(s) of each party—said procedure providing more than adequate time to

meet the Electoral College mandate. NOTE: Had
this been the law in 2000, Al Gore would be our
president, and the American economy would not
be in meltdown!

7) Finally, absent the above safeguards, and until
these safeguards are in place--Congress must
mandate that PAPER BALLOTS, ONLY, can be used
in our presidential elections. This is not a
"partisan" issue, it is a "pro-democracy" issue. Most
importantly, this will return the responsibility for
our elections, and our vote counting, back into the
hands of the individual voter, where it belongs,
and out of the hands of "corporate control"---*it is
after all "our democracy", itself, that is at risk if we
don't take these steps---and in that regard, is there
any time or cost differential that is too great?*

Reply To: Jim Green -- Democrat candidate for
Congress, Dist 21, TX, 2000
jgreen5@satx.rr.com
www.Inclusivism.org

The following is an article that appeared in the
September 1, 2004 issue of Harpers Magazine,
and it is included, here, because it should be _MUST_
reading before one is allowed to vote in the
November election. The article is enclosed in
double brackets and quotation marks—and the
irony is that while the candidates referenced at the
end are Bush II and Kerry—and the coffers at the
conservative foundations are now even more full-
-the premise is even more relevant to
Obama/Romney.

"[[TENTACLES OF RAGE: The Republican
propaganda mill, a brief history

LEWIS H LAPHAM / Harpers Magazine v.309,
n.1852, September 2004 1sep04

When, in all our history, has anyone with ideas so
bizarre, so archaic, so self-confounding, so remote
from the basic American consensus, ever got so
far? —Richard Hofstadter

In company with nearly every other historian and political journalist east of the Mississippi River in the summer of 1964, the late Richard Hofstadter saw the Republican Party's naming of Senator Barry Goldwater as its candidate in that year's presidential election as an event comparable to the arrival of the Mongol hordes at the gates of thirteenth-century Vienna. The "basic American consensus" at the time was firmly liberal in character and feeling, assured of a clear majority in both chambers of Congress as well as a sympathetic audience in the print and broadcast press. Even the National Association of Manufacturers was still aligned with the generous impulse of Franklin Roosevelt's New Deal, accepting of the proposition, as were the churches and the universities, that government must do for people what people cannot do for themselves.•

• With regard to the designation "liberal," the economist John K. Galbraith said in 1964, "Almost everyone now so describes himself." Lionel Trilling, the literary critic, observed in 1950 that "In the United States at this time, liberalism is not only the dominant but even the sole intellectual tradition." He went on to say that "there are no conservative or reactionary ideas in general circulation," merely "irritable mental gestures which seek to resemble ideas."

And yet, seemingly out of nowhere and suddenly at the rostrum of the San Francisco Cow Palace in a roar of triumphant applause, here was a cowboy-hatted herald of enlightened selfishness threatening to sack the federal city of good intentions, declaring the American government the enemy of the American people, properly understood not as the guarantor of the country's freedoms but as a syndicate of quasi-communist bureaucrats poisoning the wells of commercial enterprise with "centralized planning, red tape, rules without responsibility, and regimentation without recourse." A band played "America the

Beautiful," and in a high noon glare of klieg light the convention delegates beheld a militant captain of capitalist jihad ("Extremism in the defense of liberty is no vice!") known to favor the doctrines of forward deterrence and preemptive strike ("Let's lob a nuclear bomb into the men's room at the Kremlin"), believing that poverty was proof of bad character ("lazy, dole-happy people who want to feed on the fruits of somebody else's labor"), that the Democratic Party and the network news programs were under the direction of Marxist ballet dancers, that Mammon was another name for God.

The star-spangled oratory didn't draw much of a crowd on the autumn campaign trail. The electorate in 1964 wasn't interested in the threat of an apocalyptic future or the comforts of an imaginary past, and Goldwater's reactionary vision in the desert faded into the sunset of the November election won by Lyndon Johnson with 61 percent of the popular vote, the suburban sheriffs on their palomino ponies withdrawing to Scottsdale and Pasadena in the orderly and inoffensive manner of the Great Khan's horsemen retiring from the plains of medieval Europe.

$2 BILLION ASSETS CONSERVATIVE FOUNDATIONS (2001 ASSETS)

	(in $ Millions)
The Bradley Foundation	584
Smith Richardson Foundation	494
Scaife Family (Four Foundations)	478.4
Earhart Foundation	84
John M. Olin Foundation	71
Koch Family (Three Foundations)	68
Castle Rock (Coors) Foundation	50
JM Foundation	25
Philip M. McKenna Foundation	17.4

Departed but not disbanded. As the basic American consensus has shifted over the last thirty years from a liberal to a conservative bias, so also the senator from Arizona has come to be seen as a prophet in the western wilderness, apostle of the rich man's dream of heaven that placed Ronald Reagan in the White House in 1980 and provides the current Bush Administration with the platform on which the candidate was trundled into New York City this August with Arnold Schwarzenegger, the heavy law enforcement, and the paper elephants.• The speeches in Madison Square Garden affirmed the great truths now routinely preached from the pulpits of Fox News and the Wall Street Journal—government the problem, not the solution; the social contract a dead letter; the free market the answer to every maid-en's prayer—and while listening to the hollow rattle of the rhetorical brass and tin, I remembered the question that Hofstadter didn't stay to answer. How did a set of ideas both archaic and bizarre make its way into the center ring of the American political circus?

• The rightward movement of the country's social and political center of gravity isn't a matter of opinion or conjecture. Whether compiled by Ralph Nader or by journalists of a conservative persuasion (most recently John Micklethwait and Adrian Wooldridge in a book entitled The Right Nation) the numbers tell the same unambiguous story—one in five Americans willing to accept identity as a liberal, one in three preferring the term "conservative"; the American public content with lower levels of government spending and higher levels of economic inequality than those pertaining in any of the Western European democracies; the United States unique among the world's developed nations in its unwillingness to provide its citizens with a decent education or fully funded health care; 40 million Americans paid less than $10 an hour, 66 percent of the population earning less than $45,000 a year; 2 million people in prison, the majority of them black and Latino; the country's largest and most profitable corporations relieved of the obligation to pay an income tax; no politician permitted to stand for public office without first professing an ardent faith in God.

About the workings of the right-wing propaganda mills in Washington and New York I knew enough to know that the numbing of America's political senses didn't happen by mistake, but it wasn't until I met Rob Stein, formerly a senior adviser to the chairman of the Democratic National Committee, that I came to fully appreciate the nature and the extent of the re-education program undertaken in the early 1970s by a cadre of ultraconservative and self-mythologizing millionaires bent on rescuing the country from the hideous grasp of Satanic liberalism. To a small group of Democratic activists meeting in New York City in late February, Stein had brought thirty-eight charts diagramming the organizational structure of the Republican "Message Machine," an octopus-like network of open and hidden microphones that he described as "perhaps the most potent, independent institutionalized apparatus ever assembled in a democracy to promote one belief system."

It was an impressive presentation, in large part because Stein didn't refer to anybody as a villain, never mentioned the word "conspiracy." A lawyer who also managed a private equity investment fund—i.e., a man unintimidated by spread sheets and indifferent to the seductions of the pious left—Stein didn't begrudge the manufacturers of corporatist agitprop the successful distribution of their product in the national markets for the portentous catch-phrase and the camera-ready slogan. Having devoted several months to his search through the available documents, he was content to let the facts speak for themselves—fifty funding agencies of different dimensions and varying degrees of ideological fervor, nominally philanthropic but zealous in their common hatred of the liberal enemy, disbursing the collective sum of roughly $3 billion over a period of thirty years for the fabrication of "irritable mental gestures which seek to resemble ideas."

The effort had taken many forms—the publication of expensively purchased and cleverly promoted tracts (Milton Friedman's Free to Choose, Charles Murray's Losing Ground, Samuel Huntington's The Clash of Civilizations), a steady flow of newsletters from more than 100 captive printing presses (among them those at The Heritage Foundation, Accuracy in the Media, the American Enterprise Institute and the Center for the Study of Popular Culture), generous distributions of academic programs and visiting professorships (to Harvard, Yale, and Stanford universities), the passing along of sound-bite slanders (to Bill O'Reilly and Matt Drudge), the formulation of newspaper op-ed pieces (for the San Antonio Light and the Pittsburgh Post-Gazette as well as for the Sacramento Bee and the Washington Times). The prolonged siege of words had proved so successful in its result that on nearly every question of foreign or domestic policy in this year's presidential campaign, the frame and terms of the debate might as well have been assembled in Taiwan by Chinese child labor working from patterns furnished by the authors of ExxonMobil's annual report.

No small task and no mean feat, and as I watched Stein's diagrams take detailed form on a computer screen (the directorates of the Leadership Institute and Capital Research Center all but identical with that of The Philanthropy Roundtable, Richard Mellon Scaife's money dispatched to the Federalist Society as well as to The American Spectator), I was surprised to see so many familiar names—publications to which I'd contributed articles, individuals with whom I was acquainted—and I understood that Stein's story was one that I could corroborate, not with supplementary charts or footnotes but on the evidence of my own memory and observation.

The provenience of the Message Machine Stein
traced to the recognition on the part of the
country's corporate gentry in the late 1960s that
they lacked the intellectual means to comprehend,
much less quell or combat, the social and political
turmoil then engulfing the whole of American
society, and if I had missed Goldwater's foretelling
of an apocalyptic future in the Cow Palace, I
remembered my own encounter with the fear and
trembling of what was still known as "The
Establishment," four years later and 100 miles to
the north at the July encampment of San
Francisco's Bohemian Club. Over a period of three
weeks every summer, the 600-odd members of the
club, most of them expensive ornaments of the
American haute bourgeoisie, invite an equal
number of similarly fortunate guests to spend as
many days as their corporate calendars permit
within a grove of handsome redwood trees, there
to listen to the birdsong, interest one another in
various business opportunities, exchange

misgivings about the restlessness of the deutschmark and the yen.

In the summer of 1968 the misgivings were indistinguishable from panic. Martin Luther King had been assassinated; so had Robert Kennedy, and everywhere that anybody looked the country's institutional infrastructure, also its laws, customs, best-loved truths, and fairy tales, seemed to be collapsing into anarchy and chaos—black people rioting in the streets of Los Angeles and Detroit, American soldiers killing their officers in Vietnam, longhaired hippies stoned on drugs or drowned in the bathtubs of Bel Air, shorthaired feminists playing with explosives instead of dolls, the Scottsdale and Pasadena sheriffs' posses preparing their palomino ponies to stand firm in the face of an urban mob.

Historians revisiting in tranquility the alarums and excursions of the Age of Aquarius know that Revolution Now was neither imminent nor likely—the economy was too prosperous, the violent gestures of rebellion contained within too small a demographic, mostly rich kids who could afford the flowers and the go-go hoots—hut in the hearts of the corporate chieftains wandering among the redwood trees in the Bohemian Grove in July 1968, the fear was palpable and genuine. The croquet lawn seemed to be sliding away beneath their feet, and although they knew they were in trouble, they didn't know why. Ideas apparently mattered, and words were maybe more important than they had guessed; unfortunately, they didn't have any. The American property-holding classes tend to be embarrassingly ill at ease with concepts that don't translate promptly into money, and the beacons of conservative light shining through the liberal fog of the late 1960s didn't come up to the number of clubs in Arnold Palmer's golf bag. The company of the commercial faithful gathered on the banks of California's Russian River could look for succor to Goldwater's autobiography, The Conscience of a Conservative, to William F. Buckley's editorials in National Review, to the novels of Ayn Rand. Otherwise they were as helpless as unarmed sheepherders surrounded by a Comanche war party on the old Oklahoma frontier before the coining of the railroad and the six-gun.

The hope of their salvation found its voice in a 5,000-word manifesto written by Lewis Powell, a Richmond corporation lawyer, and circulated in August 1971 by the United States Chamber of Commerce under the heading Confidential Memorandum; Attack on the American Free Enterprise System. Soon to be appointed to the Supreme Court, lawyer Powell was a man well-known and much respected by the country's business community; within the legal profession he was regarded as a prophet. His heavy word of warning fell upon the legions of reaction with the force of Holy Scripture: "Survival of what we call the free enterprise system," he said, "lies in organization, in careful long-range planning and implementation, in consistency of action over an indefinite period of years, in the scale of financing available only through joint effort, and in the political power available only through united action and national organizations."

The venture capital for the task at hand was provided by a small sewing circle of rich philanthropists—Richard Mellon Scaife in Pittsburgh, Lynde and Harry Bradley in Milwaukee, John Olin in New York City, the Smith Richardson family in North Carolina, Joseph Coors in Denver, David and Charles Koch in Wichita— who entertained visions of an America restored to the safety of its mythological past—small towns like those seen in prints by Currier and Ives, cheerful factory workers whistling while they worked, politicians as wise as Abraham Lincoln and as brave as Teddy Roosevelt, benevolent millionaires presenting Christmas turkeys to deserving elevator operators, the sins of the flesh deported to Mexico or France. Suspicious of any fact that they hadn't known before the age of six, the wealthy saviors of the Republic also possessed large reserves of paranoia, and if the world was going rapidly to rot (as any fool could plainly see) the fault was to be found in everything and anything tainted with a stamp of liberal origin— the news media and the universities, income taxes, Warren Beatty, transfer payments to the undeserving poor, restraints of trade, Jane Fonda, low interest rates, civil liberties for unappreciative minorities, movies made in Poland, public schools.•

•The various philanthropic foundations under the control of the six families possess assets estimated in 2001 at $1.7 billion. Harry Bradley was an early and enthusiastic member of the John Birch Society; Koch Industries in the winter of 2000 agreed to pay $30 million (the largest civil fine ever imposed on a private American company under any federal environmental law) to settle claims related to 300 oil spills from its pipelines in six states.

Although small in comparison with the sums distributed by the Ford and Rockefeller foundations, the money was ideologically sound, and it was put to work leveraging additional contributions (from corporations as well as from other like-minded foundations), acquiring radio stations, newspapers, and journals of opinion, bankrolling intellectual sweatshops for the making of political and socioeconomic theory. Joseph Coors established The Heritage Foundation with an initial gift of $250,000 in 1973, the sum augmented over the next few years with $900,000 from Richard Scaife; the American Enterprise Institute was revived and fortified in the late seventies with $6 million from the Howard Pew Freedom Trust; the Cato Institute was set up by the Koch family in 1977 with a gift of $500,000. If in 1971 the friends of American free enterprise could turn for comfort to no more than seven not very competent sources of inspiration, by the end of the decade they could look to eight additional installations committed to "joint effort" and "united action." The senior officers of the Fortune 500 companies meanwhile organized the Business Roundtable, providing it by 1979 with a rich endowment for the hiring of resident scholars loyal in their opposition to the tax and antitrust laws.

The quickening construction of Santa's work-shops outside the walls of government and the academy resulted in the increased production of pamphlets, histories, monographs, and background briefings intended to bring about the ruin of the liberal idea in all of its institutionalized forms—the demonization of the liberal press, the disparagement of liberal sentiment, the destruction of liberal education—and by the time Ronald Reagan arrived in triumph at the White House in 1980 the assembly lines were operating at full capacity. Well in advance of inauguration day the Christmas elves had churned out so much paper that had they been told to do so, they could have shredded it into tickertape and welcomed the new cowboy-hatted herald of enlightened selfishness with a parade like none other ever before seen by man or beast. Unshredded, the paper was the stuff of dreams from which was made Mandate for Leadership, the "bible" presented by The Heritage Foundation to Mr. Reagan in the first days of his presidency with the thought that he might want to follow its architectural design for an America free at last from "the tyranny of the Left," rescued from the dungeons of "liberal fascism," once again a theme park built by nonunion labor along the lines of Walt Disney's gardens of synthetic Eden.

Signs of the newly minted intellectual dispensation began showing up in the offices of Harper's Magazine in 1973, the manuscripts invariably taking the form of critiques of one or another of the absurdities then making an appearance before the Washington congressional committees or touring the New York literary scene with Susan Sontag and Norman Mailer. Over a period of several years the magazine published articles and essays by authors later to become well-known apologists for the conservative creed, among them George Gilder, Michael Novak, William Tucker, and Philip Terzian; if their writing in the early seventies was remarkable both for its clarity and wit, it was because they chose topics of opportunity that were easy to find and hard to miss.

• Paul Weyrich, the first director of The Heritage Foundation, and often described by his admirers as "the Lenin of social conservatism," seldom was at a loss for a military analogy: "If your enemy has weapons systems working and is killing you with them, you'd better have weapons systems of your own."

The liberal consensus hadn't survived the loss of the Vietnam War. The subsequently sharp reduction of the country's moral and economic resources was made grimly apparent by the impeachment of Richard Nixon and the price of Arab oil, and it came to be understood that Roosevelt's New Deal was no longer on offer. Acting on generous impulse and sustained by the presumption of limitless wealth, the American people had enacted legislation reflecting their best hopes for racial equality and social justice (a.k.a. Lyndon Johnson's "Great Society"), but any further efforts at transformation clearly were going to cost a great deal more money than the voters were prepared to spend. Also a good deal more thought than the country's liberal-minded intelligentsia

were willing to attempt or eager to provide. The universities chose to amuse themselves with the crossword puzzles of French literary theory, and in the New York media salons the standard-bearers of America's political conscience were content to rest upon what they took to be their laurels, getting by with the striking of noble poses (as friends of the earth or the Dalai Lama) and the expression of worthy emotions (on behalf of persecuted fur-seals and oppressed women). The energies once contained within the nucleus of a potent idea escaped into the excitements of the style incorporated under the rubrics of Radical Chic, and the messengers bringing the good news of conservative reaction moved their gospel-singing tent show into an all but deserted public square.

NATIONAL "THINK TANKS" (2001 BUDGETS)

(in $ Millions)

The Heritage Foundation	33
American Enterprise Institute	25
Hoover Institution	25
Cato Institute	17.6
Hudson Institute	7.8
Manhattan Institute	7.2
Citizens for a Sound Economy	5.4
Reason Foundation	4.9
National Center for Policy Analysis	4.7
Competitive Enterprise Institute	3.2

Free Congress Foundation   2.7

Institute for Foreign Policy Analysis   2.5

Their chief talents were those of the pedant and
the critic, not those of the creative imagination,
but they well understood the art of merchandising
and the science of cross-promotion, and in the
middle 1970s anybody wishing to appreciate the
character and purpose of the emerging
conservative putsch could find no better
informant than Irving Kristol, then a leading
columnist for the Wall Street Journal, the author
of well-received books (On the Democratic Idea in
America and Two Cheers for Capitalism), trusted
counselor and adjunct sage at the annual meetings
of the Business Roundtable. Asa youth in the late
1930s, at a time when literary name and
reputation accrued to the accounts of the soidisant
revolutionary left, Kristol had proclaimed himself
a disciple of Leon Trotsky, but then the times
changed, the winds of fortune shifting from east to

west, and after a stint as a CIA asset in the 1950s, he had carried his pens and papers into winter quarters on the comfortably upholstered bourgeois right.

On first meeting the gentleman at a literary dinner in New York's Century Club, I remember that I was as much taken by the ease and grace of his manner as I was impressed by his obvious intelligence. A man blessed with a sense of humor, his temperament and tone of mind more nearly resembling that of a sophisticated dealer in art and antiques than that of an academic scold, he praised Harper's Magazine for its publication of Tom Wolfe's satirical pieces, also for the prominence that it had given to the essays of Senator Daniel Patrick Monahan, and I was flattered by his inclination to regard me as an editor-of-promise who might be recruited to the conservative cause, presumably as an agent in place behind enemy lines. The American system of free enterprise, he said, was being attacked by the very people whom it most enriched i.e., by the pampered children of privilege disturbing the peace of the Ivy League universities, doing lines of cocaine in Manhattan discotheques, making decadent movies in Hollywood—and the time had come to put an end to their dangerous and self-indulgent nonsense. Nobody under the age of thirty knew what anything cost, and even the senior faculty at Princeton had forgotten that it was none other than the great Winston Churchill who had said, "Cultured people are merely the glittering scum which floats upon the deep river of production."

In the course of our introductory conversation Kristol not only referred me to other old masters whom I might wish to reread (among them Plutarch, Gibbon, and Edmund Burke); he also explained something of his technique as an intellectual entrepreneur. Despite the warning cries raised by a few prescient millionaires far from the fashionable strongholds of the effeminate east, the full membership of the American oligarchy still wasn't alive to the threat of cultural insurrection, and in order to awaken the management to a proper sense of its dire peril, Kristol had been traveling the circuit of the country's corporate boardrooms, soliciting contributions given in memory of Friedrich von Hayek, encouraging the automobile companies to withdraw their advertising budgets from any media outlet that declined to echo their social and political prejudices.

"Why empower your enemies?" he said. "Why throw pearls to swine?

Although I didn't accept Kristol's invitation to what he called the "intellectual counter-revolution," I often ran across him during the next few years at various symposia addressed to the collapse of the nation's moral values, and I never failed to enjoy his company or his conversation. Among all the propagandists pointing out the conservative path to glory, Kristol seemed to me the brightest and the best, and I don't wonder that he eventually became one of the four or five principal shop stewards overseeing the labors of the Republican message machine.

It was at Kristol's suggestion that I met a number of the fund-raising people associated with the conservative program of political correctness, among them Michael Joyce, executive director in the late seventies of the Olin Foundation. We once traveled together on a plane returning to New York from a conference that Joyce had organized for a college in Michigan, and somewhere over eastern Ohio he asked whether I might want to edit a new journal of cultural opinion meant to rebut and confound the ravings of The New York Review of Books. The proposition wasn't one in which I was interested, but the terms of the offer an annual salary of $200,000, to be paid for life even in the event of my resignation or early retirement—spoke to the seriousness of the rightist intent to corner and control the national market in ideas.

• Henry Ford II expressed a similar thought on resigning as a trustee of the Ford Foundation in late 1976. Giving vent to his confusion, annoyance, and dismay, he took the trouble to write a letter to the staff of the foundation reminding them that they were associated with "a creature of capitalism." Conceding that the word might seem "shocking" to many of the people employed in the vineyards of philanthropy, Mr. Ford proceeded to his defense of the old ways and old order.

"I'm not playing the role of the hard-headed tycoon who thinks all philanthropoids are Socialists and all university professors are Communists. I'm just suggesting to the trustees and the staff that the system that makes the foundation possible very probably is worth preserving."

The work went more smoothly as soon as the Reagan Administration had settled itself in Washington around the fountains and reflecting pools of federal patronage. Another nine right-thinking foundations established offices within a short distance of Capitol Hill or the Hay-Adams hotel (most prominent among them the Federalist Society and the Center for Individual Rights); more corporations sent more money; prices improved for ideological piecework (as much as $100,000 a year for some of the brand-name scholars at Heritage and AEI), and eager converts to the various sects of the conservative faith were as thick upon the ground as maple leaves in autumn. By the end of Reagan's second term the propaganda mills were spending $100 million a year on the manufacture and sale of their product, invigorated by the sense that once again it was morning in America and redoubling their efforts to transform their large store of irritable mental gestures into brightly packaged policy objectives—

tort reform, school vouchers, less government, lower taxes, elimination of the labor unions, bigger military budgets, higher interest rates, reduced environmental regulation, privatization of social security, down-sized Medicaid and Medicare, more prisons, better surveillance, stricter law enforcement.

If production increased at a more handsome pace than might have been dreamed of by Richard Scaife or hoped for by Irving Kristol, it was because the project had been blessed by Almighty God. The Christian right had come into the corporate fold in the late 1970s. Abandoning the alliance formed with the conscience of the liberal left during the Great Depression (the years of sorrow and travail when money was not yet another name for Jesus), the merchants of spiritual salvation had come to see that their interests coincided with those of the insurance companies and the banks. The American equestrian classes were welcome to believe that slack-jawed dope addicts had fomented the cultural insurrection of the 1960s; Jerry Falwell knew that it bad been the work of Satan, Satan himself and not one of his students at the University of California, who had loosed a plague of guitarists upon the land, tempted the news media to the broadcast of continuous footage from Sodom and Gomorrah, impregnated the schools with indecent interpretations of the Bible, which then gave birth to the monster of multiculturalism that devoured the arts of learning. Together with Paul Weyrich at The Heritage Foundation, Falwell sponsored the formation of the Moral Majority in 1979, at about the same time and in much the same spirit that Pat Robertson, the Christian televangelist, sent his congregation a fundraising letter saying that feminists encourage women to "leave their husbands, kill their children, practice witchcraft, destroy capitalism and become lesbians." Before Ronald Reagan was elected to a second term the city of God signed a nonaggression pact with the temple of Mammon, their combined forces waging what came to be known as "The Culture War."

• The proposed journal appeared in 1982 as The New Criterion, promoted as a "staunch defender" of high culture, "an articulate scourge of artistic mediocrity and intellectual mendacity wherever they are found." Joyce later took over direction of the Bradley Foundation, where he proved to he as deft as Weyrich and Kristol at what the movement conservatives liked to call the wondrous alchemy of turning intellect into influence.

MASS MEDIA DISTRIBUTION

$300M CONSERVATIVE MESSAGE MACHINE

TELEVISION
Pat Robertson's 700 Club
Fox News Channel

MSNBC's Scarborough Country
Oliver North's War Stories

RADIO
The Rush Limbaugh Show
The Cal Thomas Commentary
Radio America

PUBLISHING
Eagle Publishing, Inc.
NEWSPAPERS
The Washington Times
The Wall Street journal

WEBSITES
Townhall.com
AnnCoulter.com

The Cold War against the Russians was fading into safe and nostalgic memory, and the tellers of the great American fairy tale (the one about the precious paradise ever in need of an invincible defense) found themselves in pressing need of other antagonists to take the place of the grim and harmless ogre in the northern snow.

The Japanese couldn't play the part because they were lending the United States too much money; the Colombian drug lords were too few and too well connected in Miami; Manuel Noriega failed the audition; the Arab oil cartel was broke; and the Chinese were busy making shirts for Ralph Lauren.

In the absence of enemies abroad, the protectors of the American dream at home began looking for domestic signs of moral weakness rather than foreign shows of military strength; instead of examining the dossiers of distant tyrants, they searched the local newspapers for flaws in the American character, and the surveillance satellites over Leipzig and Sevastopol were reassigned stations over metropolitan Detroit and the Hollywood studios filming Dynasty and Dallas.

Within a matter of months the conservative committees of public safety rounded up as suspects a motley crowd of specific individuals and general categories of subversive behavior and opinion—black male adolescents as well as elderly female Buddhists, the New York Times, multiculturalists of all descriptions, the 1960s, welfare mothers, homosexuals, drug criminals, illegal immigrants, performance artists. Some enemies of the state were easier to identify than others, but in all instances the reactionary tellers of the tale relied on images seen in dreams or Arnold Schwarzenegger movies rather than on the lessons of their own experience.

For a few years I continued to attend convocations sponsored by the steadily proliferating agencies of the messianic right, but although the discussions were held in increasingly opulent settings—the hotel accommodations more luxurious, better food, views of the mountains as well as the sea— by 1985 I could no longer stomach either the sanctimony or the cant. With the coming to power of the Reagan Administration most of the people on the podium or the tennis court were safely enclosed within the perimeters of orthodox opinion and government largesse, and yet they persisted in casting themselves as rebels against "the system," revolutionary idealists being hunted down like dogs by a vicious and still active liberal prosecution. The pose was as ludicrous as it was false. The leftist impulse had been dead for ten years, ever since the right-wing Democrats in Congress had sold out the liberal portfolio of President Jimmy Carter and revised the campaign-finance laws to suit the convenience of their corporate patrons. Nor did the news media present an obstacle. By 1985 the Wall Street Journal had become the newspaper of record most widely read by the people who made the decisions about the country's economic policy; the leading editorialists in the New York Times (A. M. Rosenthal, William Safire) as well as in the Washington Post (George Will, Richard Harwood, Meg Greenfield) ably defended the interests of the status quo; the vast bulk of the nation's radio talk shows (reaching roughly 80 percent of the audience) reflected a conservative bias, as did all but one or two of the television talk shows permitted to engage political topics on PBS. In the pages of the smaller journals of opinion (National Review, Commentary, The American Spectator, The National Interest, The New Criterion, The Public Interest, Policy Review, etc.) the intellectual décor, much of it paid for by the Olin and Scaife foundations, was matched to the late-Victorian tastes of Rudyard Kipling and J. P. Morgan. The voices of conscience that attracted the biggest crowds on the nation's lecture circuit were those that spoke for one or another of the parties of the right, and together with the chorus of religious broadcasts and pamphlets (among them Pat Robertson's 700 Club and the publications under the direction of Jerry Falwell and the Reverend Sun Myung Moon), they enveloped the country in an all but continuous din of stereophonic, right-wing sound.

The facts seldom intruded upon the meditations of the company seated poolside at the conferences and symposia convened to bemoan America's fall from grace, and I found it increasingly depressing to listen to prerecorded truths dribble from the mouths of writers once willing to risk the chance of thinking for themselves. Having exchanged intellectual curiosity for ideological certainty, they had forfeited their powers of observation as well as their senses of humor; no longer courageous enough to concede the possibility of error or enjoy the play of the imagination, they took an interest only in those ideas that could be made to bear the weight of solemn doctrine, and they cried up the horrors of the culture war because their employers needed an alibi for the disappearances of the country's civil liberties and a screen behind which to hide the privatization (a.k.a. the theft) of its common property—the broadcast spectrum as well as the timber, the water, and the air, the reserves of knowledge together with the mineral deposits and the laws. Sell the suckers on the notion that their "values" are at risk (abortionists escaping the nets of the Massachusetts state police, pornographers and cosmetic surgeons busily at work in Los Angeles, farm families everywhere in the Middle West becoming chattels of the welfare state) and maybe they won't notice that their pockets have been picked.

So many saviors of the republic were raising the alarm of culture war in the middle eighties that I now can't remember whether it was Bob Bartley writing in the Wall Street Journal or William Bennett speaking from his podium at the National Endowment for the Humanities who said that at Yale University the students were wallowing in the joys of sex, drugs, and Karl Marx, disporting themselves on the New Haven green in the reckless manner of nymphs and satyrs on a Grecian urn. I do remember that at one of the high-end policy institutes in Manhattan I heard the tale told by Norman Podhoretz, then the editor at Commentary, the author of several contentious books (Making It and Why We Were in Vietnam), and a rabid propagandist for all things antiliberal. What he had to say about Yale was absurd, which I happened to know because that same season I was teaching a seminar at the college. More than half the number of that year's graduating seniors had applied for work at the First Boston Corporation, and most of the students whom I'd had the chance to meet were so busy finding their way around the Monopoly board of the standard American success (figuring the angles of approach to business school, adding to the network of contacts in their Filofaxes) that they didn't have the time to waste on sexual digressions either literal or figurative. When I attempted to explain the circumstance to Podhoretz, he wouldn't hear of it. Not only was I misinformed, I was a liberal and therefore both a liar and a fool. He hadn't been in New Haven in twenty years, but he'd read William F. Buckley's book (God and Man at Yale, published in 1951), and he knew (because the judgment had been confirmed by something he'd been told by Donald Kagan in 1978) that the college was a sinkhole of depraved sophism. He knew it for a fact, knew it in the same way that Jerry Falwell knew that it was Satan who taught Barbra Streisand how to sing.

If Kristol was the most engaging of the agents provocateur whom I'd encountered on the conservative lecture circuit in the 1980s, Podhoretz was the dreariest—an apparatchik in the old Soviet sense of the word who believed everything he wished to prove and could prove everything he wished to believe, bringing his patrons whichever words might serve or please, anxious to secure a place near or at the boot of power. Unfortunately it was Podhoretz, not Kristol, who exemplified the character and tone of mind that edged the American conservative consensus ever further to the right during the decade of the 1990s.

The networks of reactionary opinion once again increased their rates of production, several additional foundations recruited to the cause, numerous activist organizations coming on line, together with new and improved media outlets (most notably Rupert Murdoch's Fox News and Weekly Standard) broadcasting the gospels according to saints Warren Harding and William McKinley. By 1994 the Conservative Political Action Conference was attracting as many as 4,000 people, half of them college students, to its annual weekend in Arlington, Virginia, there to listen to the heroes of the hour (G. Gordon Liddy, Ralph Reed, Oliver North) speak from stages wrapped in American flags. Americans for Tax Reform under the direction of Grover Norquist declared its intention to shrink the federal government to a size small enough "to drown," like one of the long-lost hippies in Bel Air, "in a bathtub."

STUDENTS AND SCHOLARS (2001 ESTIMATES)

	(in $ Millions)		
George Mason University	7		
Harvard University	6		
Intercollegiate Studies Institute	5.8		
University of Chicago		5	
Yale University		5	
Washington University			4
Stanford University		3	
Institute for Humane Studies			2.9
National Association of Scholars	1.2		

Although as comfortably at home on Capitol Hill
as in the lobbies of the corporate law firms on K
Street, and despite their having learned to suck
like newborn lambs at the teats of government
patronage (Kristol's son, William, serving as
public-relations director to Vice President Dan
Quayle; Podhoretz's son-in-law, Elliot Abrams, a
highly placed official within the Reagan
Administration subsequently indicted for criminal
misconduct), the apologists for the conservative

cause continued to pose as embattled revolutionaries at odds with the "Tyranny of the Left." The pretense guaranteed a steady flow of money from their corporate sponsors, and the unexpected election of Bill Clinton in 1992 offered them yet another chance to stab the corpse of the liberal Goliath. The smearing of the new president's name and reputation began as soon as he committed the crime of entering the White House. The American Spectator, a monthly journal financed by Richard Scaife, sent its scouts west into Arkansas to look for traces of Clinton's semen on the pine trees and the bar stools. It wasn't long before Special Prosecutor Kenneth Starr undertook his obsessive inspection of the president's bank records, soul, and penis. Summoning witnesses with the fury of a suburban Savonarola, Starr set forth on an exploration of the Ozark Mountains, questioning the natives about wooden Indians and painted women. For four years he camped in the wilderness, and even after he was allowed to examine Monica Lewinsky's lingerie drawer, his search for the weapon of mass destruction proved as futile as the one more recently conducted in Iraq.

Although unable to match Starr's prim self-righteousness, Newt Gingrich, the Republican congressman from Georgia elected speaker of the House in 1995, presented himself as another champion of virtue (a self-proclaimed "Teacher of the Rules of Civilization") willing to lead the American people out of the desolation of a liberal wasteland. Like Starr and Podhoretz (also like the newscasters who now decorate the right-wing television studios), Gingrich had a talent for bearing grudges. During his sixteen years in Congress he had acquired a reputation (not undeserved) for being nasty, brutish, and short, eventually coming to stand as the shared and shining symbol of resentment that bound together the several parties of the disaffected right—the Catholic conservatives with the Jewish neoconservatives, the libertarians with the authoritarians, the evangelical nationalists with the paranoid monetarists, Pat Robertson's Christian Coalition with the friends of the Ku Klux Klan. Within a few months of his elevation to the speaker's chair, Gingrich bestowed on his fellow-plaintiffs his Contract with America, a plan for rooting out the last vestiges

of liberal heresy in the mind of government. As mean-spirited in its particulars as the Mandate for Leadership handed to Ronald Reagan in 1980, the contract didn't become law, but it has since provided the terms of enlightened selfishness that shape and inspire the policies of the current Bush Administration.

During the course of the 1990s I did my best to keep up with the various lines of grievance developing within the several sects of the conservative remonstrance, but although I probably read as many as 2,000 presumably holy texts (Peggy Noonan's newspaper editorials and

David Gelernter's magazine articles as well as the soliloquies of Rush Limbaugh and the sermons of Robert Bork), I never learned how to make sense of the weird and too numerous inward contradictions.

EIGHT INFLUENTIAL BOOKS AND THE FOUNDATIONS WHO SPONSORED THEM

Free to Choose, Milton Friedman — Scaife Foundation Olin Foundation
The Naked Public Square, Richard John Neuhaus — Lilly Endowment Bradley Foundation Olin Foundation

The Dream and the Nightmare, Myron Magnet — Scaife Foundation

Losing Ground, Charles Murray — Olin Foundation, Smith Richardson Foundation

The Clash of Civilizations, Samuel Huntington —
Bradley Foundation, Smith Richardson Foundation

Illiberal Education, Dinesh D'Souza — Olin
Foundation

Politics, Markets &America's Schools, John E.
Chubb and Terry M. Moe — Olin Foundation

The Tragedy of American Compassion, Marvin
Olasky — Bradley Foundation

How does one reconcile the demand for small
government with the desire for an imperial army,
apply the phrases "personal initiative" and "self-
reliance" to corporation presidents utterly
dependent on the federal subsidies to the banking,
communications, and weapons industries, square
the talk of "civility" with the strong-arm methods
of Kenneth Starr and Tom DeLay, match the
warmhearted currencies of "conservative
compassion" with the cold cruelty of "the

unfettered free market," know that human life must be saved from abortionists in Boston but not from cruise missiles in Baghdad? In the glut of paper I could find no unifying or fundamental principle except a certain belief that money was good for rich people and bad for poor people. It was the only point on which all the authorities agreed, and no matter where the words were coming from (a report on federal housing, an essay on the payment of Social Security, articles on the sorrow of the slums or the wonder of the U.S. Navy) the authors invariably found the same abiding lesson in the tale—money ennobles rich people, making them strong as well as wise; money corrupts poor people, making them stupid as well as weak.

But if a set of coherent ideas was hard to find in all the sermons from the mount, what was not hard to find was the common tendency to believe in some form of transcendent truth. A religious as opposed to a secular way of thinking. Good versus Evil, right or wrong, saved or damned, with us or against us, and no light-minded trifling with doubt or ambiguity. Or, more plainly and as a young disciple of Ludwig Von Mises had said, long ago in the 1980s in one of the hospitality tents set up to welcome the conservative awakening to a conference on a beach at Hilton Head, "Our people deal in absolutes."

Just so, and more's the pity. In place of intelligence, which might tempt them to consort with wicked or insulting questions for which they don't already possess the answers, the parties of the right substitute ideology, which, although sometimes archaic and bizarre, is always virtuous.

Virtuous, but not necessarily the best means available to the running of a railroad or a war. The debacle in Iraq, like the deliberate impoverishment of the American middle class, bears witness to the shoddiness of the intellectual infrastructure on which a once democratic republic has come to stand. Morality deemed more precious than liberty; faith-based policies and initiatives ordained superior to common sense.

As long ago as 1964 even William F. Buckley understood that the thunder on the conservative right amounted to little else except the sound and fury of middle-aged infants banging silver spoons, demanding to know why they didn't have more—more toys, more time, more soup; when Buckley was asked that year what the country could expect if it so happened that Goldwater was elected president, he said, "That might be a serious problem." So it has proved, if not under the baton of the senator from Arizona then under the direction of his ideologically correct heirs and assigns. An opinion poll taken in 1964 showed 62 percent of the respondents trusting the government to do the right thing; by 1994 the number had dwindled to 19 percent. The measure can be taken as a tribute to the success of the Republican propaganda mill that for the last forty years has been grinding out the news that all government is bad, and that the word "public," in all its uses and declensions (public service, citizenship, public health, community, public park, commonwealth, public school, etc.), connotes inefficiency and waste.

The dumbing down of the public discourse follows as the day the night, and so it comes as no surprise that both candidates in this year's presidential election present themselves as embodiments of what they call "values" rather than as the proponents of an idea. Handsome images consistent with those seen in Norman Rockwell's paintings or the prints of Currier and Ives, suitable for mounting on the walls of the American Enterprise Institute, or in one of the manor houses owned by Richard Mellon Scaife, maybe somewhere behind a library sofa or over the fireplace in a dining room, but certainly in a gilded frame.]]"

ABOUT THE AUTHOR: I was employed in our Criminal Justice System for a cumulative 20 years as a probation officer, with 5 of those years as a chief probation officer. I authored the concept of "Shock Incarceration" which became law in Kansas in 1970, and then was adopted in numerous jurisdictions in the U.S. and also spread to Europe—it is currently identified in the U.S. as "Boot Camp" [as the means to "shock" the young offender—and a total distortion of my original intent—like many ideas, once released, they take on a life of their own]. I was the Democrat candidate for Congress, District 21, TX, 2000. I would most define myself as a Social Ecologist-- [albeit my degree is in Psychology]. My web page is www.Inclusivism.org –which has been on the internet since 1996.

Other books I have on Amazon/Kindle: The Harvard Boys Club, My Letters To President Obama, Letters on Steroids, and The First Time I

Had Sex [A response to the oppressive Radical Right]